Stop Selling.
Start Helping.

And Watch How Your Business Grows.

By

MATT WHITE

ISBN: 1530431344
ISBN-13: 978-1530431342

DEDICATION

This book is dedicated to all the business owners and salespeople out there who realize it's time for a change! To those who think maybe, just maybe, this whole "helping" thing just might be the real deal.

Contents

Contents

Introduction

I launched my first official entrepreneurial venture in the fifth grade: *black market reminders*.

If you're not familiar, "reminders" were given as a punishment back in the day to ensure you didn't forget what you did was wrong. So, the teacher would make you write out something like, "I will not talk in class" or "I will not run in the hallway" one hundred times on paper, or maybe on the chalkboard while the other kids got to go out to recess. (In my case, I always forgot to put my name on my papers, so I can't tell you how many times I had to write out "Matt White" on page after page after page of classic line ruled paper!)

At one time or another, almost everyone had to write reminders for some reason – "I will not talk in class," "I will not chew gum in school," "I will not hit my classmate," etc. – and everyone HATED reminders.

So, here's what I did…

I would use tape to connect four pencils together, angled slightly, so one writing action would result in four lines of written text.

Can you just picture the scene? Here's me, a fifth-grader, sitting at my desk at home with four pencils taped together, angled so I could write ONE sentence, but the output would be FOUR lines of text…

I will not talk in class.
I will not talk in class.
I will not talk in class.
I will not talk in class.

And then…I would write reminders for the other kids. I'd hit up the typical punishment phrases and have a stash of reminders ready for anyone in a pinch (I'd even change up my handwriting and use different pencils or pens to get some variety) – and then I'd charge them to buy these pre-written reminders! For those who got in trouble regularly, I created a filing system and could literally whip out a set of reminders for that kid on the spot.

At four lines of text per one time of writing a sentence, I could knock out a full page of reminders (roughly 24-25 lines if I recall) in probably 60 seconds or less. And, then I'd charge 25 cents per page – so 100 reminders would net me a buck. (*And you thought* YOUR *business idea was a good one!*)

So, what does this have to do with anything?

This book is about moving from a traditional "selling" mentality to a mindset of "helping." One of the major benefits of helping instead of selling is being a resource in such a way that, over time, you're in the right place at the right time with the right product or service. As you educate, inform and entertain your customers and prospects, you're priming the pump, so to say, for that time six months, 18 months, or two years from now when your prospect is ready to make a purchase. You don't know exactly when that will be, but your consistent presence in front of your potential customer as a helpful resource will ensure you're top of mind when they decide.

And, if done well, you can actually anticipate the needs of your audience. Whether seasonality or trends or particular pain points, you know there are certain things that trigger a higher need or desire for your content or your product or service. In fifth grade for me, it was at the moment someone got in trouble.

While I wasn't writing blogs or producing e-books to educate my fifth grade peers on the stress that's caused when a 10-year-old is forced to write reminders, I was very aware of WHO my audience was, WHAT their challenges were, and WHEN they would benefit most from my services. I never had to "sell" them anything. Word got around that I was the go-to kid in the "market!" If someone needed help, I was there to help them.

Your sales and marketing strategy should help you understand and convey to your team these very important data points as well.

Being there when your prospect is in a bind. Providing valuable information when your customers need it. Answering questions they didn't even know they had. Helping instead of selling. These are the hallmarks of a truly GREAT salesperson.

It's not going to be easy.

While reading this, you'll be forced to think differently. It's going to open your eyes to a new way to sell, without actually "selling."

If you're like me, you like to be comfortable. Change is hard. Doing things the way we've always done it is a heck of a lot easier than doing something new. But, I promise, if I can do it...you can, too!

This book is a compilation of content from more than four years of blogging about this topic.

Since January 2012, I've published more than 300 blog posts. And, here, I've pulled together some of the best and tweaked them for relevance and timeliness.

I've grouped them into "collections" that break down into the different parts of the book. Although there is an order overall, they don't necessarily flow in a linear fashion; instead, they can each stand alone, so feel free to jump around as much as you want!

Above all, I write with the same intent of the title of this book – to help rather than sell. With that being said, I hope this book helps you.

Let's get started!

Matt

PART ONE

**WHY TRADITIONAL
SALES DOESN'T WORK
ANY MORE**

MATT WHITE

Why Traditional Sales Doesn't Work Any More

Traditional sales doesn't work any more.

Did you know that more than 70% of the customer's buying decision is made before you even know he or she exists?

That's why the traditional sales process doesn't work like it used to.

In this first section, we'll discuss what's different about the buyer today and how we need to adjust in order to deal with this massive change in the buying process.

CHAPTER 1

A Tale of Two Experiences

A TALE OF TWO EXPERIENCES

I'm guessing you've probably made it to a local or regional home and garden show at least once in your lifetime. What comes to mind when you think about that experience? Close your eyes and picture the scene. I'm guessing it was NOT a relaxed, no-pressure scenario. There were likely hundreds, if not thousands, of vendors – all of them trying to grab your attention, give you a little tchotchke *(yah, that's how it's spelled! Bet you never thought about how to spell "tchotchke" before!?!)*, sell you something, or get you to sign up for something.

I'd like to share a tale of two different experiences at the imaginary local ABC Home Improvement Show...

The first experience goes like this...(imagine you're the consumer for a minute)

You're excited for the Home Show this year because you've decided to remodel your kitchen some time in the next 12 months or so, and you're looking forward to learning a lot and possibly connecting with someone who can help.

You walked by my booth (let's pretend I'm a home remodeler), and I was lucky enough to get your attention and have a short conversation with you about your kitchen and some of the ideas you have. We chat a little bit, and you're kind enough to share your email with me so I can follow up with you after the show. You move along with the rest of your day at the show – interacting with several other remodelers.

Then, a day or two after the show, you get an email from me with a link to an article I wrote that relates to the very situation you explained to me at the show. No selling, just offering a helpful article based on our conversation – something that provides a little information to help in your research.

A few days later, you get a postcard in the mail with a link to download a free e-book that shares the "Top 10 Things to Consider When Remodeling Your Kitchen." Along with the e-book download, there's an option to request a free consultation in your home; but you're not quite ready to jump in just yet. You're still gathering information.

Ten days pass by, and you receive another email from me with a note to check in and a link to another blog or video that relates to your kitchen project. No pressure, no urgency to act. Just helpful information and an offer to talk more if you'd like.

How are you feeling right about now?

Now, the second experience is quite different...

It starts the same. You walk by my booth, and I was lucky enough to get your attention.

But, this time I pressure you out of the isle for a minute to hear what I have to say. We're giving away a free iPad, so that's where I begin. "Fill out this form to be entered to win a free iPad," I explain.

I ask if you've got any plans to make changes in your home soon, and you share a little about your upcoming kitchen remodel plans. I tell you about the discounts we're offering if you start your project by the end of the month; and you say you're not quite ready to start yet, but you fill out the form for the iPad drawing. You figure, "Why not?"

A week later, you receive an email offering a discount on all remodeling services, as long as you begin your project by the end of the month. You ignore the email because you're not ready to jump in just yet. You're still gathering information.

A week later, you get another email offering an even bigger discount and an urgent message that says the offer will disappear if you don't respond in two days. You have to "click here" to schedule an appointment right away!

You unsubscribe and delete the email.

Which version did you like? Which one made you feel better? Which one built credibility with you as the consumer?

Interruption vs. Engagement

This scenario can play out in any number of ways – not just for remodelers at home shows. The difference is engagement versus interruption. Effective marketing today is focused on engagement, not just trying to sell you my stuff, but rather trying to help you make the best decision for your particular situation.

Interruption isn't valued. But engagement is.

JOE PULIZZI
ContentMarketingInstitute.com

Is your marketing engaging, or are you following the old-school selling model of interruption?

If you're stuck in the "interruption" mode of marketing, it's time to make a change. Customers are buying differently. No matter what business you're in, **HELPING IS THE NEW SELLING.**

CHAPTER 2

What are We Teaching Our Kids?

WHAT ARE WE TEACHING OUR KIDS?

I came across this scene in our garage one late spring day...

Since the weather in Ohio had FINALLY taken a positive turn, my youngest son, Ian (9 at the time), and a friend had set up a lemonade stand.

And, in case you need a translation, it says, "Fifth customer gets their lemonade free."

As I read this, I had two thoughts:

1. "Great thinking, kid. That's my boy – following in his dad's marketing footsteps!"
2. "What in the world are we teaching our kids?"

At first, I was proud of his creative thinking and marketing prowess. At such an early age, to figure out that creating an "offer" often helps to drive sales is pretty impressive, I think. (I may be a little biased!) And, it's true, offers like this *can* generate interest, give you something specific to focus on, and ultimately increase sales.

My second thought was this: while there's nothing wrong with special offers, discounts and teasers, depending on them for the long run can be detrimental. (Okay, maybe not so much for my son, but for businesses, in general!) I realized that "we" – society – are teaching our kids that FREE, DISCOUNTED, BUY-ONE-GET-ONE, or any other offer is the ONLY way to get people to buy our stuff.

We're teaching them that "salesmanship" is all about providing your product or service at a discount (or even free) in order to get someone to buy.

So, what if Ian had done the opposite?

What if, instead of offering the fifth customer a free lemonade, his sign said, "Nana's Old-Fashioned Lemonade" and with every cup sold, they gave away a little notecard with Nana's Old-Fashioned Lemonade recipe on it? Then, I bet they could charge $1.00 rather than 50 cents. They wouldn't have to give anything away, and they'd double their revenue!

Instead of discounting, they'd be providing added value.

Rather than cheapening their product, they'd be increasing its value.

Free, discounts, and other offers DO work sometimes.

But, what if you didn't HAVE to give away your products or services?

What if you could actually charge full price…or even *increase* your price?

What if you offered so much value through your product or service that people would be willing to pay almost anything for it? When you educate, inform, and entertain, beyond just producing a great product, you build credibility and increase interest.

So, let's stop discounting our products and services. Instead, let's offer more value, more information, more help.

Maybe I'm being a little tough on Ian; he was only nine!

But, just so you know, I did NOT take away his iPad because he focused too much on discounting his product and not enough on offering value!

It just got me thinking…that's all.

—— **CHAPTER 3** ——

Pulling vs. Pushing: A Sales Methodology That Works

PULLING VS. PUSHING:
A SALES METHODOLOGY THAT WORKS

Have you ever tried to push a string?

It doesn't work. It bends under your pressure. It folds the minute you begin to push.

So, if you had to move a string, what would you do? You'd pull it, right? You could even tie something to the end of that string and pull it along, too.

Now, imagine your prospect as a string.

Pushing her won't do you any good. So, consider pulling instead.

Sandler Sales Training CEO Dave Mattson is quoted as saying, "The Sandler sales methodology reflects a conversational sales model, with a 'pull' process instead of a 'push' process. Most salespeople throw a great deal of product knowledge at their potential customers, while the Sandler sales methodology focuses on pulling people in, using their knowledge of the product throughout the buying process."

(I'll share my bias here – I'm a huge fan of Sandler Sales Training. As of this writing, I've been involved with Sandler for nearly five years; and it's made a huge difference in my business over that time.)

Why pulling works better.

Before I started with Sandler, my mentality going into a sales meeting was, "I need to sell them a website." Sure, I'd ask some questions to find out what they might need, but the goal was absolutely to get the prospect to buy something from me. **Walking away without the sale meant I failed.**

So, I pushed. I pushed that string as hard as I could. And, sometimes it would work. They might be in the perfect situation and really needed what I had to sell. I wasn't "pushy" in an annoying way, but my goal was to get to the sale.

As I began to learn the Sandler concepts, my whole mindset changed. This idea that we are to "pull" our prospects along (in a positive way, not a manipulating way) made a big difference. When we focus on uncovering their pain, understanding the impact that pain is having, and recognizing that we can help, we don't have to "push" our product or service on the prospect; instead, both parties see there's a fit and work together to create a solution.

Pulling allows for a "No."

In the same interview referenced above, Dave Mattson added, "The Sandler sales methodology also gives salespeople the ability to receive a "No" when and if there is no clear ROI – if the numbers don't add up, then it's okay to accept that there is no fit."

Another concept that made a major impact on my mentality in the sales process was this idea of "No" being okay. Rather than feeling rejected if the prospect didn't need, or even want, what we offered, I realized we were not a fit for everyone.

Even when we're approaching the conversation with a "pull" focus, sometimes our solution isn't the answer, or they can't afford our services, or there just might not be a fit for whatever reason. And that's okay.

When we're pushing, though, a "No" is hardly ever acceptable. If our only possible outcome is a "Yes," and we push as hard as necessary to get there, the prospect feels pressured, and we often make promises we can't (or shouldn't) make in order to get the business.

Think of your prospect as a string.

So, next time you're talking with a prospect, think of them as a string; pushing won't do any good. Instead, consider pulling them…ask questions, understand their situation, and recognize whether or not you can really help. If you can, tell them you can; and if it's not a good fit, be honest and let them know.

—— **CHAPTER 4** ——

Traditional Sales is Like French Kissing a Total Stranger

TRADITIONAL SALES IS LIKE FRENCH KISSING A TOTAL STRANGER

"Hello. I know we just met, but can we make out?"

This is basically what you're saying to your prospects when you try to get them to buy your product without educating them as to WHY your product is the answer, or even IF your product will help solve their problem.

So, back to the conversation…

"Hello. I know we just met, but can we make out? No? Well, did I tell you I'm 5' 7" and weigh 160 pounds? I was born in Martinsville, VA, and have two brothers. I went to Kent State University and studied advertising. I lived in Greenville, SC, for about four years and moved back to Ohio in 1999. Now, can we make out?"

Seriously. If they didn't bite right away (which I'm guessing they didn't), this is the next thing you tell your prospects with your PowerPoint deck, your About Us page or maybe your Product Specifications page on your website…company background; product features and benefits; photos of the machines that make your products.

Your audience doesn't care about all that crap. *(More on that later!)*

Educating helps them understand.

Rather than pushing your products and services, consider producing content that will HELP your prospects?

- Instead of asking for a kiss (to buy your product/service), try asking and answering some questions.
- Instead of sharing all the details about your product, try sharing testimonials, or "third-party stories," from others in their same situation who have benefited from your product.
- Instead of detailing the company history, try telling the story of your company's impact on the industry. *(More on telling stories later, too!)*

Valuable content helps your prospect make a connection. It helps them uncover the pain themselves. And it builds credibility for you and your organization.

Don't force the French kiss on the first date!

Get to know your prospect a little more first.

CHAPTER 5

Lemonade for Sale

MATT WHITE

LEMONADE FOR SALE

I'm going to finish this section with another story about lemonade. This time, it was our middle son, Isaac's story. He was 10 at the time...

Our neighborhood has an annual garage sale that has grown to something of a spectacle. The 'hood has about 250 homes in it, and probably 20% of them participate – 50 houses in a neighborhood garage sale is C.R.A.Z.Y., let me tell you. People parking in every possible open spot (fire hydrant or not); police are called every year, and tickets are given out; even though the big sign out front clearly says 9am-3pm, people are hovering outside our garages at around 7:30! Truly an experience.

While it's our goal to get rid of the junk we've collected over the years (amazing how we can ALL have more junk to sell year after year!), our kids have begun to figure out it's also an opportunity for them to capitalize on the captive audience of thousands of people coming through the neighborhood over these two days.

Isaac had been looking forward to that year's garage sale for months. Not only does he LOVE buying things, but he also enjoys SELLING things and MAKING money. Besides the stack of things he gathered from his room to sell, he was also excited to open a lemonade stand. About two  months prior, he had created a sign to really grab people's attention!

So, the day came, and as Isaac (and his younger brother, Ian) was setting up his stand, we all noticed the neighbors directly across the street were also setting up a lemonade stand! The competition had begun!

Shortly after Isaac finished setting up shop, another neighbor from down the street joined Isaac and Ian, bringing brownies to sell, too! (The "competition" across the street was selling cookies!) Along with the brownies came the neighbor boy and his three friends (all teenagers). Isaac was very overwhelmed with these boys; they took over some of his selling space; they had sandwich boards made up and were walking around, yelling, "Brownies for sale. Delicious brownies for sale. Come get your brownies!" Meanwhile, Isaac sat there and poured cup after cup for people who continued to come up asking for lemonade. He took their money kindly, with a "thank you."

At one point, the "competition" started calling out what they had…"Lemonade. Cookies. Popsicles. Juice boxes. Come and get it!" One of the teenage boys who had joined Isaac's team started saying things like, "Their cookies are laced with poison." or "You can drink their lemonade, but you should know, it was made by the devil, himself." (I thought that one was particularly funny!) Meanwhile, Isaac continued to sell lemonade, quietly and consistently.

One woman walked up, and the older boys went about their "selling" ways – spouting off one of the bashing comments of the cookies being sold across the street (I think it was the devil reference). The woman said, "I was planning on buying one of your brownies, but now I'm not so sure. You need to tell me why I should buy your brownies, not why I *shouldn't* buy your competitor's cookies." (We learned soon after that she had been in sales for 30 years and was prepared to teach a lesson to these boys!)

Ultimately, she got the one boy, in particular, who had been making the bashing comments to "sell" her on their brownies. He started with, "They're perfect." She dug for more. "They're delicious and melt in your mouth." Still not sold. "They were made with love and compassion." THAT got her going. "Now you're speaking my language," she said. She did end up buying a brownie. (And, she bought a cookie from across the street!)

Meanwhile, Isaac kept on pouring lemonade (although he was definitely paying attention to the conversation going on between the lady and the older boys).

The big lesson...

Isaac was in the right place (tons of people walked by that day) at the right time (it was about 88 degrees) and he provided a product that met the needs of the target audience (refreshment on a hot day). There was no hard sell coming from his mouth, outside of the random call of "Lemonade for sale. 25 cents." He wasn't forcing something on people that they didn't want or need. He wasn't talking poorly about the competitors. He just offered a great product and met a need.

Although they got bored after just a couple hours, Isaac made $12.75 (that's more than 50 cups of lemonade sold). I don't know how much the older boys made on their brownies, but I'm pretty sure they ate most of the profits!

PART TWO

A NEW SYSTEM FOR
BUYING MEANS A NEW
SYSTEM FOR SELLING

A New System for Buying
Means a New System for Selling

People have so many options today. As explained in the entire first section, the traditional sales process just doesn't cut it any more.

Because of that 70 percent number referenced earlier, as salespeople, marketers and business owners, we have to reach our audience earlier than we ever have. We must engage with them when that initial 70 percent of the buying decision is being established.

"Content Marketing" is a relatively new phrase used in sales and marketing today. The authority in content marketing is the Content Marketing Institute (CMI). Yes, that's an actual thing; and if you're in sales or marketing, you NEED to know about CMI! (http://www.contentmarketinginstitute.com.)

CMI defines content marketing this way:

> *Content marketing is the marketing and business process for creating and distributing relevant and valuable content to attract, acquire, and engage a clearly defined and understood target audience – with the objective of driving profitable customer action.*

Content marketing is exactly what will help you deal with this new buyer's system. The concept itself is not new; it started decades ago when some companies realized, even way back then, that buyers prefer to buy from people they know, like and trust. And, in order to build that feeling of "know, like and trust," there has to be some level of HELPING involved in the conversation – not just a transaction.

—— **CHAPTER 6** ——

How Content Marketing is Bringing Sexy Back

HOW CONTENT MARKETING IS BRINGING SEXY BACK

Justin Timberlake's got nothin' on content marketing!

As of the writing of this book, one of our business-to-business clients has seen an increase in organic search traffic by more than 1,400 percent in 18 months and has driven more than 200 new "actions" from organic search traffic alone.

Now, THAT is sexy!

What's driving these huge improvements? Content marketing. Specifically, generating targeted, relevant, optimized blogs, combined with premium "gated" content, and focused email-marketing efforts.

Many people still have a hard time understanding what "content marketing" is. I try to explain it in a variety of different ways, but the simplest definition is this: *Content marketing is about helping, rather than just selling.*

And, helping has never been so sexy!

I speak on this subject across the country, and I love the reaction every time…

- *"That makes sense."*
- *"I never thought of it that way."*
- *"This could be huge in our business."*
- *"That's different than what my competition is doing."*
- *"I could see it working like…"*

Effective content marketing looks something like this…

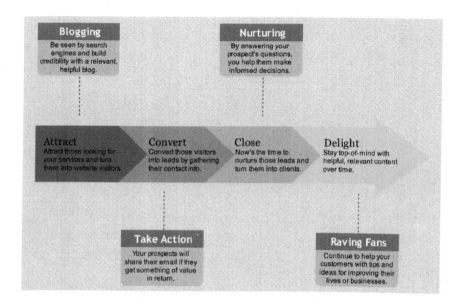

This example above is specific to online marketing, but this idea of content marketing, or helping instead of selling, can and does truly walk someone through the buying process, just without the traditional sales mentality:

1. **Consumers want to get educated** – before making a purchase, buyers have to start somewhere; often this involves a visit to the web and/or a physical location.
2. **Buyers ask questions** – buyers inevitably have questions as they move through the buying process; and every company – B2B or B2C – has an opportunity to answer their questions.
3. **They will consider their options** – deeper into the buying process, it becomes a matter of comparison or detailed consideration: Why should I purchase from you versus someone else?
4. **Then, and only then, will they make a Decision** – finally, it's decision time; and almost always a decision is made on an emotional level, so trust and credibility are vital – it's rarely just about price.

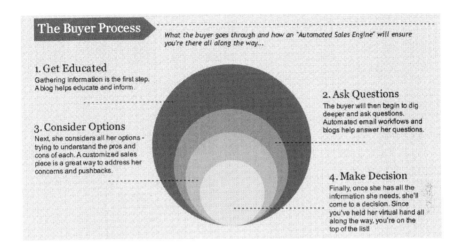

So, where does this sexiness begin?

At JoltCMS, we call it a Content Marketing Blueprint (http://www.joltcms.com/blueprint) – and it is exactly what the name conveys: a blueprint for an organization's content marketing efforts, and it often bleeds over into general online and offline marketing, too.

- It defines your target audience in great detail.
- It uncovers those things that trigger your prospects to want to get educated.
- It answers the questions they have.
- It establishes a foundation for your messaging.
- It connects your prospect's online experience with your offline sales process.
- It builds a specific plan to attract, convert, close, and delight your audience.

Whether or not you think your business or product is actually sexy, content marketing can bring sexy back to your messaging and relationship with your prospects and customers!

It's proven to work and can do the same for you.

CHAPTER 7

Let's Talk About Me for a Minute

LET'S TALK ABOUT ME
FOR A MINUTE

"Let's talk about me for a minute."

Would you ever start a conversation that way? (Don't answer that. Let's just pretend you wouldn't.)

Do a little exercise for me: Open up your company's proposal. Open up your PowerPoint presentation. Look at the home page of your website. Think about your "30-second commercial."

What do the first few slides/paragraphs/statements look like?

"We're in 57 countries. We offer 14 different products. We've been around since 1982. We work with ABC, XYZ and QRS companies. Our products are better than any other products out there."

Sound familiar? **Well, people don't care.**

Sorry. It's just the truth. Okay, maybe they care a little bit. But that's not the #1 thing on their mind.

So, what IS on their mind?

- I'm frustrated with _____.
- I need help with _____.
- I don't understand _____.
- I'm stressed about _____.
- I don't have time to deal with _____.
- I'm not even sure WHAT would help me. I'm just trying to figure things out.

Next time you give a presentation, share a proposal, go on a sales call, whatever…do me a favor. Leave behind the PowerPoint slides that brag all about you and your company.

Instead, bring a list of questions that will help your customer/prospect/audience express what it is that THEY want out of the discussion. Be genuine about wanting to help, not to just "sell" them something.

Seriously. Do this.

Then let me know how it goes. Email me at matt@joltcms.com.

Buyers have questions. Answer them.

The following was pulled from a NYTimes.com article published in 2013. It's the story of Marcus Sheridan, who at the time was owner of River Pools & Spas. The title of the article was "A Revolutionary Marketing Strategy: Answer Customers' Questions."

It is an indelible image of the financial crisis: a bird's-eye view of the backyards of foreclosed houses, their in-ground pools festering with algae and mosquitoes. In Northern Virginia, Marcus Sheridan was in the financial storm.

By early 2009, his company, River Pools and Spas, a 20-employee installer of in-ground fiberglass pools in Virginia and Maryland, had a decline in orders from an average of six a month to barely two. That winter, four customers who had planned to install pools costing more than $50,000 each demanded their deposits back. For three consecutive weeks, the company overdrew its bank account.

Around this time, Mr. Sheridan began to overhaul his marketing. The company had been spending about $250,000 a year on radio, television and pay-per-click advertising. It would now cut the budget to about a tenth of that and focus on generating sales through informational blog posts and videos, what has become known as content marketing. But Mr. Sheridan took an unconventional approach to his content.

As a result, River Pools has recovered to exceed its peak pre-2007 revenue, and Mr. Sheridan, a 35-year-old father of four, has become something of a Web marketing guru. While he still owns a 33 percent interest in the pool company, his partners manage it day to day while he concentrates on his new venture, TheSalesLion.com. He recently spoke about his marketing approach in a conversation that has been edited and condensed.

Q. *Take us back. How did you save your company?*

A. I just started thinking more about the way I use the Internet. Most of the time when I type in a search, I'm looking for an answer to a specific question. The problem in my industry, and a lot of industries, is you don't get a lot of great search results because most businesses don't want to give answers; they want to talk about their company. So I realized that if I was willing to answer all these questions that people have about fiberglass pools, we might have a chance to pull this out.

Q. *What was the first question you answered?*

A. The question I was always asked within the first two minutes of talking to customers was, How much does a fiberglass pool cost? Pool installers are like mattress or car dealers — we hate talking about how much a pool costs until we have you in person because there are so many options and accessories we want to sell you. As a result, pool companies never mention price on their Web sites. But I said, I don't care what the question is, we're going to answer it.

Q. *Did you actually tell people the price of a pool?*

A. No — because I couldn't. But see, that's the magic behind this. Google's search engine doesn't really care if we answer the question. It's just looking for companies that are willing to address the question. So I said in that article, there are a ton of options, so it depends, the price can range anywhere from $20,000 to $200,000 and a lot of our customers end up between $40,000 and $80,000. And that was enough. Within about 24 hours of writing that article, it was No. 1 for every fiberglass-pool, cost-related phrase you could possibly type in. And because I have analytics, so far to this day, I've been able to track a minimum of $1.7 million in sales to that one article.

Q. *What was the next question?*

A. People used to ask me all the time, "Marcus, I've been hearing that fiberglass pools have all sorts of problems and issues. So what are the problems and issues?" Of course, they'd been talking to a concrete pool guy, but it doesn't matter where they got it, now they have the question. So we wrote an article about the problems with fiberglass pools and specifically came right out and said: Here are the issues. Here are the benefits. You decide. Now, when you go in and type anything about fiberglass issues and problems, you're going to see the River Pools Web site and you're going to think, "Oh my gosh, these guys are so honest."

Q. *Anything else?*

A. In most industries, there comes a time in the sale process where the customer turns to you and says, "O.K., I like you, but who are some of the other good companies that do this?" Half the time it's a test, because people know who our competitors are because they can find them in .5 seconds online. Most contractors avoid the question. They say, "Oh, we don't really have competition." But because I was asked that question so often, I decided to answer it. I wrote a blog post about the best swimming pool builders in Richmond, Va., one of our main service areas.

Q. *Where were you on the list?*

A. I wasn't on it.

Q. *You weren't?*

A. No, because the moment I put my name up there I would lose all my credibility. But here's the thing. Take the first company on the list, Pla-Mor Pools, a top competitor of ours. If you type in, "Pla-Mor Pools reviews Richmond, Va.," which of course people do all the time when they're vetting a company, what comes up? *Me!* You vet all my competitors, now I'm showing up for all their key words. If you really want to understand the power of inbound marketing, it comes down to this idea: I want to have the conversation at my house.

Q. *Once you wrote a blog post, how much time did you spend promoting it on Twitter and Facebook?*

A. I didn't. Dude, that one article on price has never been tweeted. It's never been Facebooked. I'm not saying social media doesn't help, but it's nowhere near what people think. The only metric that really matters is total pages viewed. Here's a statistic for you: If somebody reads 30 pages of my River Pools Web site, and we go on a sales appointment, they buy 80 percent of the time. The industry average for sales appointments is 10 percent. So, our whole marketing campaign revolves around getting people to stick around and read our stuff, because the longer they stay on our site, the greater the chance they're going to fall in love with our company.

Q. *What do you say to business owners who say they don't know what to blog about?*

A. That's the dumbest thing I ever heard, and I hear it a lot. What they should be doing is just listening to every single question they get and answering it. In my consulting business the first thing we do is brainstorm what questions the company gets on a regular basis. I've never had a company come up with less than 100 questions in 30 minutes.

Q. *How do you suggest companies find time to do all of this blogging?*

A. Most of the time, they can take the employees they already have talking to customers and turn them into content producers. If you have 25 salespeople, and each one of them writes one post a month, your search is going to be through the roof because that's a new piece of content every day.

Q. *How have your competitors responded to all of this?*

A. They still don't really get it. They're nice about it. I'll have one of my best-pool-builder lists come out, and I'll run into them. And they'll say, "Hey, man, thanks for including me in that list. I'm not sure why you did it, but thanks."

Mark Cohen, "A Revolutionary Marketing Strategy: Answer Customers' Questions," *NYTimes.com*, The New York Times, February 27, 2013.

CHAPTER 8

Not Everyone is a Good Fit to be Your Customer

NOT EVERYONE IS A GOOD FIT
TO BE YOUR CUSTOMER

I hate country music.

Being raised in Texas, you might think otherwise; but I cannot stand it. At my annual "Guys Weekend" trip a few years ago, we shared control of the music selection, each of us connecting to the Bluetooth speaker at different times.

My brother-in-law (we'll call him "Mike") took control at one point. Before I knew it, he went from some great 90's alternative to "today's country."

Blah.

After probably 15 twangin' songs about losing dogs and girlfriends, I was just seconds away from cutting my own ears off to stop the madness! I finally stole back the DJ spot and immediately pushed some Jay Z into the speaker.

Ahhh…relief.

My hatred toward country music (and the love Mike has for it) is proof that some things are just meant to work together. For me and country music, this is NOT the case.

The same is true in business.

When I'm meeting with a prospect for the first time, my goal is NOT to "sell" them something. My goal is to find out if what we're good at is a fit for what they need. And, in many instances, it's not. Usually, I'll know it before they do.

At Jolt, here are the four things that will tell me right away if we're not going to be a good fit…

1. The #1 question is, "What does it cost?"

If price is the biggest issue, we're not the right partner. We know we're not the cheapest. We also know we're not the most expensive. I believe you get what you pay for; and what we do, we do well. I'm always very open about our pricing. It is what it is.

2. There's a three-quote RFP process.

Somewhat connected to #1, if there's a Request for Proposal (RFP) process, we're typically not the one that ends up on top. In my opinion, RFPs are 97% based on price – even though most claim the decision is based on several factors. If it's all about the RFP, how can someone know if the people on both sides of the project will get along? How do they know whether there are additional elements that should be considered? An RFP process, for our industry anyway, is a flawed process.

3. The expectation of content marketing, SEO and/or social media is to drive business immediately.

It's a cheesy comparison, but what we do is closer to a marathon than a sprint. Or, like the Tortoise and the Hare, it takes focus and time and effort to win. Each client is different, and although we don't usually get into long, locked-in contracts, we do stress that what we do takes time. If someone is looking for overnight success, we're not going to be a good fit.

4. The meeting is 100% about business.

If you're familiar with the DISC profile system, you'll know exactly what I'm talking when I say I'm a "high S". DISC is a personality assessment tool. S stands for "Steadiness" – it's all about cooperating, being patient, and listening; but it's also about valuing loyalty and helping others. When I meet someone for the first time, I want to get to know him or her personally. I want to understand where they're coming from, what's their biggest challenge, why they are where they are, etc. If the only interest is talking business, there are plenty of folks out there who don't care for the personal relationship and just want to "get it done" – that's not us. We are truly interested in creating success for our clients, and for that to happen, we have to know what "success" looks like, deep down and not just surface level success.

We're not a fit for everyone, and we know this. The sooner we find this out, the better for all involved.

The same is true in your business. There are some clients who are better clients. There are some who just don't fit. Don't take on a client just because they have money. Take on a client because you KNOW you can help them.

Take on a client because it's a great fit!

MATT WHITE

PART THREE

NO ONE CARES

No One Cares

Get over yourself. No one cares.

Seriously. No one actually cares about your product or service.

People only care what it/you will do for them...

> *Will you solve my problem?*

> *Will you help me?*

(And, in some cases, *Will it make me feel good?*)

When your audience comes in contact with your business, **do you help solve their problems better than anyone else in the world?** (Thanks, Marcus Sheridan – aka @TheSalesLion – for this little question! We'll get to that question soon enough.)

Well, do you?

CHAPTER 9

One Question You Should Be Asking Yourself

ONE QUESTION YOU SHOULD
BE ASKING YOURSELF

As I just mentioned, when it comes down to it, there's really just one question that should drive your sales and marketing efforts.

"When people (visit my website, talk with my salespeople, come in contact with our brand, etc.), *do we help solve their problems better than anyone in the world?"*

Dang. That's a great question, right?

Hard to hear the answer, though, if we're being truthful. But, in an age where people can get information from all kinds of sources, if you want to genuinely lead your industry, the answer to this question HAS to be "yes."

I love Jay Baer's concept of "Youtility" (http://www.youtility.com) …the idea that you need to be a valuable resource for your clients and prospects. He says it like this:

> *"The objective is not to make information. The objective of content marketing is to produce information that customers and prospective customers* **will use.**"

So, for example, when people visit your website, do you help solve their problems better than anyone in the world?

If not, what's the purpose of your website?

If not, what are people going to walk away with when they visit your website?

If not, maybe you shouldn't even have a website at all?

That last one may seem a little harsh, but think about it. If all you do is provide information about your product, bios of your staff, pictures of your product...but you're not *helping solve your prospect's problems*, they'll move on to the next company who will.

Seriously, how did you answer the question?

"When people (visit my website, talk with my salespeople, come in contact with our brand, etc.), *do we help solve their problems better than anyone in the world?*"

If your marketing and sales efforts aren't helping your customers and prospects improve their own lives and businesses by answering their questions and solving their problems, you're missing out on an opportunity to 1) help more people and 2) grow your business beyond your wildest imagination.

Helping is the new selling. And you'll be left behind if you don't embrace this fact.

CHAPTER 10

The Most Difficult Thing About this Concept

THE MOST DIFFICULT THING ABOUT THIS CONCEPT

You know what I've found to be the hardest thing for business owners when it comes to helping versus selling?

Here's a quick reminder of the definition of "content marketing":

> *Content marketing is the marketing and business process for creating and distributing relevant and valuable content to attract, acquire, and engage a clearly defined and understood target audience – with the objective of driving profitable customer action.*

So, what's the hardest part of that definition to implement?

"RELEVANT and VALUABLE"

Myself included, as small business owners, we're all about attracting, acquiring and engaging; and we're especially fond of "driving profitable customer action," right?

The challenge is in making our content **relevant and valuable** to the customer or prospect. We can talk about our products and services all day long. We can spew features and benefits out the wazoo! We can produce a great sales video or write an awesome introduction about a new product or service.

Truly effective content marketing has the goal of **being genuinely relevant and valuable to your audience.** What this means for you will vary. It could mean talking about what your product DOES NOT do. It could mean a side-by-side comparison of your service and a competitor's. It could mean addressing something that's not specifically connected to your product, but rather a related topic your audience would find helpful or interesting.

When you're trying to help more than sell, the biggest question should always be: *Is this relevant to our audience?*

If you can answer that question in the positive, you're heading in the right direction.

— **CHAPTER 11** —

3 Questions that will Change Everything

THREE QUESTIONS THAT WILL CHANGE EVERYTHING

Want to break down content marketing into its simplest form? The concept of "Youtility" from Jay Baer's book by that name (http://www.youtility.com) all comes down to a few simple questions.

If you can answer these three questions, it will change everything!

1. Who is your ideal customer?
2. What do they need?
3. How can you help?

Seriously. That's it.

Okay, there's a little more, but it's just details from this point. You may have multiple personas (ideal customers), and they may need a lot of different things; and you may be able to help them in a variety of ways.

The tough part is narrowing down your focus. I'm amazed how often I get an answer to the first question - Who is your ideal customer? - that sounds something like this:

"Well, we do X for _____, _____, _____ and sometimes _____. We can really work with all these types of people/companies. Oh, and we also do Y for _____ and _____."

I actually asked a new client this question recently in a written questionnaire. "Who is your ideal customer, your ideal audience?"

His answer: "future customers."

Come on! You're killin' me!

Often times, it takes an outsider to look at your situation from another perspective. I love it when I'm talking with someone about their business and the opportunities that exist for them, and then an idea comes up and they say, "I've never thought of that before. I'm gonna write that down."

Following up on the new client I referenced above, after a while, he came around to understanding my question better. And, what originally started as four primary audiences turned into five once we talked through how each targeted audience's needs and challenges are different. An audience they used to consider one, was actually two distinctly unique groups, each with its own "persona."

Remember, no one cares about your product or service. They only care HOW your product or service will help them. Focus on that, and you're miles ahead of your competition – and in a great position with your prospect.

PART FOUR

POSITIONING YOURSELF AS THE EXPERT

Positioning Yourself as the Expert

Do you have a hobby or passion? I'm talking outside of work. Do you love tinkering with old cars? Are you a competitive mountain biker? Do you spend your free time scuba diving or ballroom dancing?

What do you do to learn more about this passion? How do you get better? Certainly, you practice or spend time "doing" it. But, what else? Do you read blogs or magazines about the topic? Do you go to trade shows or conferences to stay on top of the latest trends surrounding your passion? Are there certain "experts" who are the go-to people when comes to everything related to the category?

Can you be that expert to your prospects and customers?

I have a friend and client named LeCharles Bentley. He is a former NFL and Pro Bowl offensive lineman who was one of my very first clients when I started JoltCMS in 2009. At the time, there was no one in the offensive line community who had really become the stand-out expert in the field.

LeCharles saw an opportunity to become that expert. It did not happen overnight. When he started, he couldn't even get high school coaches to return his calls. But, he stuck to it. We built an online platform called O-Line World where members could watch educational videos and read articles all about the offensive line.

Today, LeCharles runs an exclusive, invitation-only offensive line training camp for NFL players; he's got a partnership deal with Nike; he has developed several products for offensive line training; and we recently helped him launch www.lbolineperformance.com, a website that's become THE authority for everything related to the O-line.

It took several years, but LeCharles is the perfect example of positioning yourself as the expert. And, you can do it, too.

— CHAPTER 12 —

Why You Shouldn't Worry About the Competition

WHY YOU SHOULDN'T WORRY ABOUT THE COMPETITION

There are a lot of great companies out there in your industry, and they're doing really good work for their clients. How much do you pay attention to them?

Whatever it is, that's too much! (Unless you said none at all.)

When I get asked about our competition, I always struggle to answer. I guess, ultimately, we do "compete" with other content marketing, website design or SEO companies, but rarely do we consider who we're "up against." That's not to sound cocky, but rather just confident, I suppose.

It's all about finding the right fit.

Let me explain. When I meet with someone to discuss their online marketing (or even general business) challenges, my goal is NOT to sell them our services. **My goal is to find out if their problem is a good fit for our solution.**

There's a bit of wordplay in that last phrase, but it's crucial to notice – I'm not trying to figure out if they can use our services; instead, I know what we do works in a few specific situations, so I'm listening for THAT particular problem/situation to come up in conversation, and then we can talk through what we do and how it can address that specific problem.

For my company, JoltCMS, it may come up in a variety of ways, but the "problem" we're ultimately looking for sounds something like this:

"We're struggling to use the web to drive sales."

This is the problem that's a perfect fit for our solution: a content marketing plan and the tactical implementation to fulfill that plan.

It could be that they struggle with driving traffic to their website; it could be a concern about online engagement and ongoing communication with prospects and leads; or it could be an issue with converting those leads into sales. Any of those "triggers" will lead a prospect right into the arms of our solution.

And, at this point, the competition doesn't matter. I have uncovered the specific pain/challenge/issue the prospect is dealing with; I've revealed it's impact on the company, and on the prospect herself; and I've helped her understand that what she's struggling with is the EXACT thing that we are awesome at addressing. Competition? What competition?

What is that phrase/pain point you're looking for? What is the perfect problem that fits just right with what you're great at?

Many times, we're not a good fit, and that's okay. We only want to do business with people who truly need what we offer, who see the value in what we do and can help them with. We're not trying to "sell" anything; rather we're trying to determine if we can help.

And THAT is why we don't worry about the competition. If we can help, that's great. If someone else would be a better fit, then that's better for the prospect, and that's great, too.

Go Give

I have read *The Go-Giver* at least 10 times. I can never get enough of this book…or more so, the concept of the book. Bob Burg and David Man do an awesome job of presenting what they call, "A Little Story About a Powerful Business Idea."

If you have not read this book, stop whatever you're doing right now and go buy it (http://amzn.to/1Uvk4so) and start reading it as soon as possible. Even if it means putting this book down for a minute!

When I read it the last time, one thing I noticed was the various examples/characters in the book and the different businesses they each represent. It really shows that the "Go-Giver mentality" spreads across every possible business and life situation.

Whether you're a restaurant owner, the CEO of a large company, an insurance agent, a sales rep, or whatever, the "Five Laws of Stratospheric Success" will apply in one way or another:

1. **The Law of Value:**
   Your true worth is determined by how much more you give in value than you take in payment.
2. **The Law of Compensation:**
   Your income is determined by how many people you serve and how well you serve them.
3. **The Law of Influence:**
   Your influence is determined by how abundantly you place other people's interests first.
4. **The Law of Authenticity:**
   The most valuable gift you have to offer is yourself.
5. **The Law of Receptivity:**
   The key to effective giving is to stay open to receiving.

Like I said, go buy this book now. (http://amzn.to/1Uvk4so)

— **CHAPTER 13** —

The Power of Personal Presence

MATT WHITE

THE POWER OF PERSONAL PRESENCE

Are you old enough to remember the TV show, *Happy Days?* Does the name Arthur Fonzarelli ring a bell? Remember when "The Fonz" would walk into a room? (If you don't know who I'm talking about, check this out: http://bit.ly/1nHrRVd)

Talk about "personal presence." That dude had personal presence.

What defines personal presence in Fonzie's terms?

- When he walks into a room, heads turn.
- Conversations open up to include him.
- When he speaks, people listen.
- When he leads, people follow.

The Fonz had confidence. He had a style. He brought an air into the room when he entered.

Do you have that? Is your mindset "I have a million dollars in the bank and I don't need the business?" Are you convinced you have the cure for your industry's cancer?

Or do you carry around the weight of the world? Are your shoulders slouched and head hung low? Is your attitude driven by the response your prospect gives you? A "yes" and you're flying high…a "no" and we're scraping you off the floor?

While your personal presence has a lot to do with your physical presence, it's often more about your self-belief (or self-doubt).

Whether you know it or not, your thoughts – the attitude, the head trash, the doubts, the questions – are coming across loud and clear to the person across the table.

When you love your product…when you can't wait to get up in the morning to talk with more people about your product…when you genuinely believe you have the cure for your industry's cancer, there's nothing that can stop you!

And, truthfully, it won't matter what you're wearing or what type of briefcase you carry or car you drive, your personal presence is driven from the inside out. That confidence comes out and fills the room. People recognize it. They want it.

Only YOU can determine your personal presence. Starting with your thoughts and beliefs, personal presence emanates through your pores.

And, the people around you will notice.

We're Awesome! Buy Something!

What's the point of your website?

Are you presenting a message of credibility, expertise and helpfulness? Or does your website scream this: "We're awesome! Buy something."

Go look at your website right now. Seriously. Get online and pull up your website – then come back here and continue on…

(Do it. For real.)

Okay…now, back to it.

Ask yourself these three questions:

> 1. What's the very first message you see when you open the page?
> 2. Does that message address a problem or question your ideal client has?
> 3. Why not?

(That third question makes an assumption. If the answer to #2 was YES, then you're in a better place than most. Congratulations!)

But, most likely, that's not the case. I'd say 90 percent of the websites out there focus on one of the following as their core message out of the gate...

- Product highlight
- Client testimonial
- News about the company
- Current offers or promotions
- "Who We Are/What We Do" of some sort

Who cares?

I mean that literally. Who cares about your product? Who cares about your latest press release? Who cares if I can get $100 off if I buy before the end of the month?

People are selfish.

What they really want to know when they visit your website is whether or not you can help them. Can you solve their problem? Will you answer their questions?

If that doesn't come across in the first few seconds of visiting your website, you lose. They click out and move on to the next one.

— CHAPTER 14 —

5 Reasons Why You Lost that Sale Last Week

5 REASONS WHY YOU LOST THAT SALE LAST WEEK

How was your close rate last week? 100 percent? Probably not. How about 80 percent? No? 50? 20? Ummm, five?

If you're like most salespeople (or business owners involved in sales), you were likely on the lower end of that scale, for sure. Achieving a 20 to 30 percent close rate is considered strong, compared to the average.

However, did you know if you just changed a few things, you could improve that percentage in a big way?

It's not rocket science, but it does involve a change in mentality. Since adjusting my own mindset around sales and business after I began with Sandler Sales Training (http://bit.ly/1SLiMHY), I've seen close rates of anywhere from 50 to 80 percent in a given month.

What if half of everyone you met with became a client? Imagine how much time you'd save. Think about the commission or income this would generate for you and/or your company!

Here are five reasons why you didn't convert more of those prospects into clients…and what you can do to improve.

Mistake #1: No established expertise

Think back to one of those opportunities lost. How were you perceived before you even walked in the door? Did Mrs. Prospect have a preconceived idea of what you could do for her? Or, did you walk in and have to start from scratch to build credibility?

<u>Two things you can do here.</u>

1. First, position yourself as an expert in your industry. One way you can do this is through social media – for example, using LinkedIn to share knowledge and relevant information your prospects and customers can use, or regularly writing a blog that addresses trends and topics in your industry. It's likely Mrs. Prospect did a little research on you before you came in for the meeting. If your LinkedIn profile hadn't been updated since May 2009, that says something about you!

2. Second, send "homework" before the meeting. One of the most effective tactics I've implemented over the last couple years is to send a short questionnaire to the prospect prior to getting together. This will be different for everyone, but you can see what ours looks like: http://www.joltcms.com/sample-homework (PW: "homework").

The goal is to gather some valuable information BEFORE you walk into the meeting. This can include as few as five questions or it can go much deeper; your product/service or industry will determine what you need to address in yours. The homework process does three things: 1) gathers valuable information, 2) gets you prepared for the meeting and 3) shows the client you're on top of things!

If you take nothing else from this book…take this! Send homework.

Mistake #2: No expectations for the meeting

Did your meeting start with something like this from Mrs. Prospect:

"I'm looking for someone to get me this widget for under $50. Can you do that?" (or some variation of this)

This puts you in a defensive mode from the start, doesn't it? Don't feel bad. It's how most first-time conversations start. But, it doesn't have to be that way.

Next time this happens, here's what you say: *"Possibly. But, can we take a step back for a minute?"* Then, I want you to address four points:

1. **Time:** Confirm how much time you have. (Hopefully, this was set prior to the meeting, and you're just reiterating.)

2. **Her Agenda:** Find out what's on her mind – when your time is up, what does she need in order to feel like it was a good meeting?

3. **Your Agenda:** Share your agenda – what do you hope will come of the meeting?

4. **Outcome:** Discuss next steps. There are three options that could happen at the end of your time together: Yes, no or a clear next step (The idea is for your prospect to understand that some kind of decision will need to be made today. It might be that there's a good fit and moving forward is logical. It's also possible there will NOT be a fit, and that's okay. Or it may be best to take some other step – schedule a follow up meeting, etc.)

Assuming you sent over a few homework questions, the second and third points above should just be a review to confirm nothing has changed since the meeting was scheduled.

Setting expectations up front is crucial. If you're not clear about these things, you can't be upset when it doesn't end up moving in the one direction or another.

Let's pretend you performed steps one and two effectively. Your reputation as an expert preceded you, so credibility was established before the meeting began. And, as you started the meeting, a clear set of expectations was agreed upon. Now, it's time to find out if you can help Mrs. Prospect.

Mistake #3: Didn't dig deep enough

The goal at this point is to discover what her "pain" is. But, it's not just surface-level pain; you want to dig deeper and learn what's truly causing that pain. For example, she may say that her current provider has been raising his prices, so she's looking for another option because it costs too much now. On the surface, this sounds like her pain is related to price. But, by just asking one more question, you can learn a lot.

Try something like this: *"When you told him you thought his price was too high, what did he say?"*

She probably wasn't ready for this question, and it'll force her to go a little deeper. She might tell you she hasn't brought it up with him, or she may say he told her there was nothing he could do about it. Either answer could lead to another question. If she hasn't brought it up, you could ask why not. If the current provider said price was out of his control, you could ask how that made her feel. In either case, you're digging deeper to learn more about her pain.

Let's say she hasn't brought it up with him yet, and when you ask why, she shares that there have been some customer service issues recently, so when the price increased, it gave her a reason to start looking at other options. And, now you're getting to the real problem – customer service.

Mistake #4: Budget wasn't clear

Ever get to a point in a new business conversation where you think, *This is a no-brainer?* You're confident this one is a done deal. And then you start discussing budget and everything goes South!

"I didn't realize it would be that much," comes back from Mrs. Prospect.

If you run into this one often, you should bring up budget/price earlier in the conversation, possibly even when you're setting expectations for the meeting.

"Mrs. Prospect, one thing I want to get out on the table right away is that our widget can cost anywhere from $40 to $100. As we begin our conversation, I want to make sure you know where we stand on price."

Price can even be addressed as early as the homework step (mentioned earlier) – it can be completely straightforward and listed as budget levels to select (we recently started including specific price ranges in our homework). The goal is to get the prospect thinking about budget before you walk in the door.

Mistake #5: Talking with the wrong person

Here's another question: When you get to the end of your discussion, and everything seems to be moving along well, does Mrs. Prospect say, "Okay. Great. I just need to share this with Bob and Stacy, and we should be good to go."

While this may sound like a good "next step," it's actually one of the worst things that can happen on a sales call. You've spent a good 45-50 minutes learning, asking questions, discussing options…and then you find out that the person you're talking to isn't the final decision maker! Now, you have to start all over when you get in front of Bob and Stacy…if you're lucky enough to get in front of them!

Another point that can be addressed when setting expectations for the meeting is to understand who the key players are and what the decision-making process is for the company. It's better to find out early on that Bob and Stacy will need to be pulled in, rather than be surprised with this information at the end of a meeting.

Ideally, when you find out others are involved in the decision process, you could ask that those people be brought into the meeting today. But, if that's not possible, this knowledge will help as you go through the process with Mrs. Prospect today. You can ask questions like, *"How do you think Bob would feel about that?"* Or *"Does Stacy deal with those same issues?"*

This is another point that can be addressed in your homework. We ask the question: *"Who else besides yourself will be involved in the decision making process?"*

So, which one of these mistakes got you?

You may be able to jump all over these five mistakes, starting tomorrow! Or, these concepts may take some time to put into practice. Taking one at a time is probably best. Start with one and see how it goes. Then, over time, begin to apply these other tactics one by one.

Ultimately, you are meeting with Mrs. Prospect because you think you can help her. Avoiding these mistakes will ensure you get to that point a lot quicker.

Get Rich. Target a Niche.

If you needed heart surgery, which one would you choose…a general practice doctor or a heart surgeon?

If you wanted to learn how to drive a race car, which one would you choose…a driver's education instructor or a performance driving school?

If you wanted great sushi, which one would you choose…a bar and grill that serves sushi or a sushi bar?

Be something to someone.

It's very difficult to be everything to everyone. It's harder to fulfill; it's harder to promote; it's harder to stand out.

But, if you can be "something to someone" instead of "everything to everyone," that's when you can shine.

I think I also heard the quote "Get rich; target a niche." from Drew Davis. It's the same concept as the quote above. Focus your efforts on one particular audience, and you will be more successful.

What's your niche?

So, what's your niche? Who is your best customer? What area of your business do you have the most fun? Make the most money?

MATT WHITE

— CHAPTER 15 —

Shortening the Sales Cycle: Five Tips to Reduce the Time from Lead to Sale

MATT WHITE

SHORTENING THE SALES CYCLE: 5 TIPS TO REDUCE THE TIME FROM LEAD TO SALE

Are you frustrated with the typically long selling cycle in the your industry? Would you like to stop wasting your time with unqualified prospects? Would you like to improve your overall close rate?

I'm guessing the answer to all those questions is a resounding YES!

People don't like to be sold.

Before we get into the five tips, I want to make sure we're clear on one core belief: **people do not like to be sold.** Can we agree on that?

Consumers are bombarded with marketing (and sales) messages thousands of times every day. We are overwhelmed with ads on Facebook, commercials on TV, billboards as we drive, advertising on the radio…everywhere we go, we're "sold" on something.

In order to stand out from the sea of sameness – to rise above the marketing smack-down that most other businesses follow – you have to act differently.

You have to help instead of sell.

What people want is to be helped. They want to have their questions answered, their problems solved, their concerns dealt with.

And this is where these five helpful marketing tips come into play.

1. Talk about money.

People care about money. It is almost always on the top of their mind – even if budget isn't the number one concern, your customer will still need to know how much the project is going to cost.

So, why wait to talk about it? Why not address it early on in the conversation?

Most of us were brought up to believe it's not polite to talk about money, and we've carried that belief with us into adulthood. But, money is a big part of what you do; and whether you're the most expensive guy in your market or you're priced pretty competitively, money is going to come up.

2. Use online quoting tools.

Along with talking about money, as recommended in the first tip, this second suggestion is closely related. I realize for most this is a very scary topic, and putting pricing online is often considered a no-no. But, stick with me a minute…

I'm not asking you to quote a full project online without ever talking to a prospect. What I'm suggesting is that you provide more opportunities for your prospects to "self-qualify" prior to you having to spend time with them.

This can be as basic as a spreadsheet that shares average investment levels for your products and/or services, including ranges for good, better, best. Or it can be as detailed as a fully automated calculator the prospect fills out in order to calculate a range based on her specific needs and wants.

The point here is to make it easy for your prospect to understand what's involved when it comes to your price. There's nothing more frustrating – either for you or your prospect – than to go through the entire quote/proposal process and find you're not even close when it comes to budget.

3. Pre-Appointment Content

I'd highly recommend if you're going to start with implementing just one of these five tips, this one should be your first.

Before your first appointment with the prospect, you have the perfect opportunity to set the stage – to define your process, to share your expectations, to define outcomes, etc. You are the expert, and this is where you have the biggest chance to stand out.

As I mentioned before, we call this pre-appointment content "homework" and it can make all the difference in the world. You likely have a list of questions you hope to address in your initial sales call or appointment. What if you knew those answers BEFORE you went into that first call?

I suggest sending a set of questions to your prospect before your first meeting, and requiring the prospect to provide answers before you meet. Let's pretend you're a remodeler; your homework form might ask questions like the following:

- What made you decide to consider renovating your kitchen/bath/basement?
- How long have you been thinking about this project?
- What's your budget?
- When would you like to have the project completed?
- Do you already have a design in mind?
- What's your biggest concern going into this project?
- Who else, besides yourself, will be involved in making decisions?

Armed with this information, you will be able to make a few decisions prior to the call – 1) is this a good fit for your company, 2) should you reach out to the prospect to address any concerns, or 3) is it in your, and the prospect's, best interest if you cancel the meeting?

How does canceling a meeting help speed up the sales cycle? Well, if you don't have to waste time on what would have been a bad meeting anyway, isn't that getting you to a decision faster? And, for those you do meet with, there's less room for miscommunication and misunderstanding from the get-go, ensuring less time between consideration and decision.

Want to see an example of real homework form in action? Check out http://www.joltcms.com/sample-homework (password: homework).

4. Promote Familiarity

I recently heard about a doctor who calls all his new patients the weekend before their initial visit. True story. The doctor will take a list home of the first-time patients who are on the schedule for the following week. He'll take a few minutes on Saturday or Sunday to make a quick call to introduce himself, tell them he's looking forward to meeting them, and ask if they have any questions before their visit.

Can you imagine getting that call? Talk about standing out from the crowd!

If you're like many businesses, you are likely one of a few companies your prospect is meeting with. How might you build familiarity with the prospect to show her you're different than the others?

- Place a call a day or two prior to the appointment.
- Send a link to a website page with your salesperson's (or your) photo and quick story of what he loves best about working at your company.
- Send an email with a link to a video of the salesperson (or yourself), making a brief introduction and sharing a little about himself.

Create a connection before that first meeting by familiarizing the prospect with you and/or your team. It'll go a long way.

5. Resolve concerns before & after the first appointment

If I had to guess, I'd say you could give me a list of common questions/concerns that come up almost every time you meet with someone new. How much will it cost? How long does it take? What's your process? What makes your widget different?

As with the money question in tip #1, why not address these questions/concerns before they even come up?

Come up with – or have your sales team come up with – the top ten questions you hear regularly during the sales process. Then, write a blog article or create a short video addressing each one and publish them on your website. Once these are created, you can use them throughout the sales process – send prior to a meeting as part of the homework or send as a follow up based on something that came up in the conversation.

When you answer her questions/concerns, you build trust with your prospect. Others may be able to answer on the fly, but when you can point to an existing piece of content, it shows your prospect she's not alone...you've dealt with her concern before.

MATT WHITE

— CHAPTER 16 —

It's About Being Human

IT'S ABOUT BEING HUMAN

When you think about it, this whole "helping vs. selling" thing should come naturally for most generally kind, good people. Most human beings *want* to be a resource for others; they *want* to do what's right; they *want* to help people.

Here, I summarize a couple different articles from others in the industry that hit this very point.

Humanize your brand.

The first, a blog on Moz.com from **Mackenzie Folgelson** and **Mathew Sweezey** called "4 Ways to Build Trust and Humanize Your Brand," (http://bit.ly/1DhsQ0e) is quite possibly the best blog post I've ever read on content marketing. To summarize the four points...

1. **Build an Emotional Connection:** "More than a great product or service, it's the passion and cause at the core of the company that builds this much deeper emotional connection between the brand and the customer."
2. **Listen and Respond with Action:** "When you truly listen to someone, you gain their trust, and more importantly, their respect."
3. **Put the Relationship Ahead of Conversions: "The key to** creating content that will convert is to optimize for the relationship with the consumer, not the conversion."
4. **Deliver on Your Promises:** "How you deliver on your promise dictates what happens next: do you build a relationship or do you lose a fan?"

What does all this boil down to? One thing: *being human.* This is exactly how we would expect a good person to act. A friend who lives by these four concepts is a GREAT friend.

Speaking Human

The other article that struck me was one I read recently in *Chief Content Officer* magazine (http://bit.ly/1cqoaGW) entitled, "Speaking Human." In it, authors Kevin Lund and Eileen Sutton address the struggle with most businesses when it comes to content marketing – selling too much!

Three points made in the section called "How to Speak Human" help shed some light on what it takes to really connect with people – just be human!

- **Tell stories:** "Unless you have a real story, loyalty is out the window."
- **Be humble:** "Don't sell me a camera. Teach me how to take great pictures."
- **Be relevant:** "Cast too wide a net, and the meaning of your content marketing is lost."

I've already shared the formal definition a couple times in this book, but Lund and Sutton summarized content marketing very succinctly at the end of the article…

"Above all, consider how you can be genuinely useful to clients and make their days and lives better."

And that's what it comes down to. It's not a difficult concept – helping others. But, it's often difficult to implement as a business that has always been focused on SELLING stuff. The purchase will still be the end result. But, **content builds trust; trust builds relationships; and relationships drive revenue.**

PART FIVE

WHAT DOES THIS LOOK LIKE ONLINE?

What Does This Look Like Online?

So, I've talked about all these great benefits of helping versus selling. Now, how do you put this into action on the web?

I will explain the "online sales funnel" in the next chapter, which is the primary process of implementing a strategy of helping online; but the idea here is to take this new attitude you've been reading about up to now, and apply it online.

However, there's more to it than just being helpful online.

It's about taking all these concepts we've already touched on…

- Pulling vs. Pushing
- Answering Questions
- Establishing Credibility
- Concentrating on the Customer, not Yourself
- Focusing on a Niche
- Telling Relevant Stories

…and putting them into action on your website, in your emails, through social media, with e-books and videos, webinars and podcasts. The same overall experience your prospects and customers have with you offline should happen online.

MATT WHITE

— **CHAPTER 17** —

What Does an Online Sales Funnel Look Like?

MATT WHITE

WHAT DOES AN ONLINE SALES FUNNEL LOOK LIKE?

I often get asked...

"What does content marketing have to do with sales?"

Or...

"Why are you talking about sales? I thought you were a web guy."

The truth is, the two go hand in hand. As I referenced earlier, the end result of content marketing is to "drive profitable action." So, there is a direct correlation between content marketing and sales.

When we build a content marketing plan, the goal is two-fold:

1. Help our clients gain a complete understanding of where their opportunities for sales are.
2. Provide a detailed plan to take advantage of those opportunities.

That detailed plan comes in the form of specific recommendations for content creation (including blog topic suggestions, e-book ideas and more), calls-to-action, landing pages, lead nurturing emails, re-engagement activities, and ultimately conversion plans as well as a way to track and measure it all.

Basically, it establishes a "sales funnel" online. Like this...

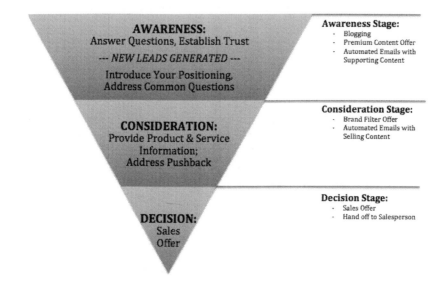

It looks a lot like a typical sales funnel...

- Attract
- Engage
- Nurture
- Sell
- Deliver

Only it's modified for the web, like this...

- Attract
- Convert
- Close
- Delight

An online sales funnel takes the idea of *Stop Selling. Start Helping.* and automates the process for the web. In very general terms, it works like this:

- Create content that attracts the right visitors to your site (blogs, videos, e-books, etc.)

- Give them something of value through that content (helpful tips, resources they can use, "secrets" to success, etc.)
- Ask for a small investment in exchange for more valuable content – not necessarily money, but rather an email address or other piece of information
- Continue to provide more valuable content over time, leading the recipient toward another "action" (could be a purchase or maybe just a link to another helpful piece of content)
- Build credibility over time as an industry expert – provide more helpful information
- Become top-of-mind for your prospects when they need your product or service (or know someone who does)
- Repeat!

Business owners, especially in business-to-business, tend to look at the web as a different beast altogether. "We have our sales guys, and we have our website."

What's missing is the connection between the two.

MATT WHITE

— **CHAPTER 18** —

Why Your Online Marketing is Failing

WHY YOUR
ONLINE MARKETING
IS FAILING

Are you frustrated because your online marketing efforts don't seem to be producing results? Are you putting in the time and effort, but your website still isn't generating quality leads?

Well, I'm going to share with you seven reasons why your online marketing is failing...

1. It's all about you.

Think about the last time you visited a website. Were you excited to see a photo of the office building on the home page? Did you love all the "we" statements you noticed as you read through the text:

- "We've been around for 47 years."
- "We manufacture ABC widgets."
- "We offer the highest quality products."
- "We help organizations solve problems."
- "We are experts in XYZ."
- "We...we...we...we...we!"

I'm guessing the answer is, NO, those things didn't jump out to you as helpful. Think about that for your online marketing, as well. Is it all about you and your company and your products or services? How many "we" statements do you see on your home page, in your email newsletter, or in your blog?

I've said this already, but I'll say it again, people are selfish. They don't care about your company – or even your product; they want to know if you can help them. Will your product solve their problem? Can they trust you with their money? Will visiting your website get them closer to resolving their current challenge?

Helpful tip:
Ask yourself this one question – When people visit our website, do we solve their problems better than anyone else in the world? (See Chapter 9)

2. You're not talking to the right person.

Who is your best customer? I'm talking about the ONE, ideal customer – the one that if you had 10 or 100 of her, you'd be enjoying life, making more money than you need, and providing the perfect solution that meets and exceeds expectations for her every single time.

Does your online marketing "speak" to this person?

> You can't be everything to everyone; but you can be something to someone.
>
> **ANDREW DAVIS**
> www.akadrewdavis.com

Well-known marketing expert, Andrew Davis, says "You can't be everything to everyone; but you can be something to someone."

Confession time: We struggle a lot with this one! Most companies do. But, it's 100 percent true – you can get rich when you target a niche. (See call-out section after Chapter 14)

Helpful tip:
Define your ideal customer. Check out this article from Content Marketing Institute for help. (http://bit.ly/1OvDPvD)

3. You're not in the right place.

Are you marketing on Facebook? Do you have an Instagram

account? How about LinkedIn, Twitter, Tumbler, or YouTube? Are you sending out emails? Do you produce e-books or infographics?

None of these is right. And none is wrong, either. Just because a channel exists doesn't mean you need to be there.

The question to ask is, *"Where does our audience get its content? And, in what format do our customers/prospects consume that content?"*

I could share a thousand different examples to make this clear, but I won't do that. I'll simply say this: Your specific audience absolutely has a preference when it comes to its choice of online channels and types of content it will engage with. Find out what those are and make sure you're there.

Helpful tip:
Do the research. As with the buyer persona article referenced above, you need to learn WHERE your customers hang out and HOW to use that platform to reach them.

4. There's nothing interesting, entertaining or educational.

Do your blog titles grab attention? Does your website make people want to stick around? When someone leaves your site, are they feeling good about what they just read, saw, heard, or experienced?

One of the questions we ask during the content marketing planning process is, *"How can I create interesting yet consistent content that will attract new customers and retain old ones?"*

The key here is "interesting" and "consistent."

Every piece of content in your online marketing program must be interesting and consistent; otherwise, no one will care, no one will share, and no one will buy.

Helpful tip:
Consider these 100 blogging ideas from Chris Brogan: http://bit.ly/1yne30V They are creative and thought provoking –

both for yourself and your customers/prospects.

5. You're only concerned with selling stuff.

In general, people don't want to be sold; they want to be helped. There's a reason you avoid "that guy" at the Chamber meetings, ignore that "unknown" number coming through on your phone, or tell the salesperson at the clothing store, "I'm just looking."

We want to make educated buying decisions and feel like we did the right thing. When you help your prospects, instead of focusing on selling something to them, everyone wins. Your prospect understands better. You build credibility with her. Whether she buys right now isn't the real bottom line. If she feels helped, she'll remember that; she'll tell someone about it; and, at some point, she's likely to buy something if it's truly what she needs/wants.

Helpful tip:
Review your content – your website, your email newsletter, your blog, your product information. Is it helpful? Or are you just selling?

6. Your website sucks.

When it comes to success or failure in online marketing, often it comes down to your website. I wrote a blog about this one – "14 Reasons Your Website Probably Sucks." (http://bit.ly/1QQ1DKI)

Helpful tip:
Check out that link above. Read it and act on it!

7. There's no call-to-action.

#2 on that list of reasons your site sucks is, "Your website has NO call-to-action." Yes, it's a specific reason your website might suck; but it's also worth mentioning in more detail here.

What specific action do you want your website visitors to take? Do you have one? Do you have too many? This one pulls together many of the others in this list: the right audience, the right platform, educational/helpful content. If all these things are in place, but there's no clear action to be taken, then all the other efforts are useless.

Once a visitor lands on your website, why should she stay? You've got about 10 seconds to give her a good reason to stick around! If you're not 100% clear on WHY she should pay attention, she is 100% likely to click away to find another website/business that is. Visitors need to know right away what it is you do and how you can help them.

Helpful tip:
Check out Day #9 of our free "30 Days to Website Success" program (http://bit.ly/1TZiT4q). It's called "Clarity Trumps Persuasion." and addresses this particular point. Sign up for the full 30-day program at http://bit.ly/1Urg2Q1.

So, what are you going to do about it?

If your online marketing isn't producing the results you expected, hopefully these seven points will help you re-evaluate your online marketing activities and re-energize you and your team to keep at it, but with a more targeted effort.

— **CHAPTER 19** —

What Does Content Marketing Have to Do with Sales?

WHAT DOES CONTENT MARKETING HAVE TO DO WITH SALES?

I was talking with a new friend/business connection recently. He had heard me say something about "helping versus selling," and he was a little confused.

I'll paraphrase:

> "I see that you talk a lot about sales. What's the connection between sales and what you do? You're a web guy, right?"

Sometimes we get lost in our own world when it comes to the terminology we use to explain what we do, don't we? And, this question spurred me to think about the way I explain what "content marketing" is and how it relates to an organization's bottom line.

I've referenced this already a couple times, but here's that definition again of content marketing from the Content Marketing Institute:

> *Content marketing is the marketing and business process for creating and distributing relevant and valuable content to attract, acquire, and engage a clearly defined and understood target audience – with the objective of driving profitable customer action.*

Read that last line again: *"with the objective of driving profitable customer action"*

Now, I had already talked with this guy about what JoltCMS does – content marketing, website design, search engine optimization, etc. – so he knew all that. But, where I had failed was making the direct connection between these activities and sales – the bottom line.

Content Marketing and Sales

At its core, the goal of content marketing (as with any form of marketing) is to DRIVE SALES.

When you produce an e-book/video/white paper/blog post/etc. that helps your prospect or customer avoid typical mistakes, for example, the goal is to give them valuable content which, in turn, builds credibility which, in turn, increases the likelihood they'll buy from you at some point in the future.

This is a very simplified version of how this works, but hopefully you get the point: content marketing and sales should go hand in hand.

A WARNING:

Here's the tricky part...while your content marketing is ultimately intended to drive "profitable customer action," you must still produce content with the genuine attitude of HELPING; not solely for the purpose of selling. If not, your prospects and customers will see right through it.

In fact, this is what I love so much about what we do. I hate sales. (See call-out on next page.) But, what I love is helping people.

When I can help people AND drive "profitable customer action," that's when it all clicks.

I Hate Sales.

That statement has probably spewed from my mouth more times than Lindsay Lohan has been on the cover of a gossip magazine!

The ironic thing about this statement is that it still applies, even after several years of involvement with Sandler Sales Training and running my own businesses.

So, why is that?

Our revenue doubled in my first year with Sandler. A couple years later, in 2014, we nearly doubled again.

And, I'll tell anyone who's willing to listen that it has **EVERYTHING** to do with Sandler and changing my mentality around sales.

So, how can I still say, "I hate sales?"

Because I don't consider it "sales" anymore.

Here's what "sales" used to look like for me (in my mind at least):

- "I don't want to be a bother, so I won't make that phone call."
- "What if they don't want what I'm selling?"
- "I *have* to do a proposal; it's what they asked for."
- "I can't charge that much."
- "If someone needs my services, they'll find me."

All those thoughts came from the basic belief that I was trying to push my services on people, whether they wanted or needed it. I honestly believed that we did great work, but it felt like I was there just to "sell" them something.

What made the difference was this:

"I'm not here to sell you anything. I'm here to find out if we can help solve your problems and grow your business."

For me, THIS is what was missing. So, now I don't look at it as "sales." I just see it as helping people.

I still hate sales in the traditional sense of the word. But, what I love is helping – and what I've found is that when you're there to **sell**, people put up walls, barriers, fronts, etc.

But, when you're there to **help**, they open up and allow you to understand their situation and you can both decide whether or not there's a fit.

MATT WHITE

Just Be Useful

I mentioned Jay Baer earlier. He's the author of *Youtility*. I'm not sure if it's a quote from the book or one I grabbed from his blog, video series or podcast at ConvinceandConvert.com, but he says, "Just be useful."

It's a pretty basic concept, but one that hits right at the center of everything I've talked about in this book.

Just be useful.

Dictionary.com defines useful like this: "being of use or service; serving some purpose; advantageous, or of good effect; of practical use."

Being useful means getting beyond your product or service and actually considering the human being on the other side of the table. What is bothering her? What challenge is he facing? What frustration is she dealing with? Is there something you can do to help?

MATT WHITE

— **CHAPTER 20** —

Give It Away! Content Marketing is About Giving

GIVE IT AWAY!
CONTENT MARKETING
IS ABOUT GIVING

"Why in the world would I give away all our knowledge for free?"

I'm going to pull a piece of brilliance here from Joe Pulizzi's book, *Epic Content Marketing*. He answers that question this way:

> *"As the great Don Schultz has always said, communication is the only true competitive advantage. If you don't help your customers reach greater heights, who will? Your competitors?"*

Think about it this way…

- o Do you want to position yourself as the expert in your field? Give away your knowledge.
- o Do you want to show how you're leading the industry in thinking and innovation? Give away your knowledge.
- o Do you want to be recognized as the go-to source for doing what you do? Give away your knowledge.

Make it clear that you know what you're talking about. Don't hide it and assume people will "get it" by looking at your product-focused website or leave-behind brochure!

- o Do you have a process you go through? Share it.
- o Do you have a specific pricing structure? Share it.
- o Do you have suggestions that could improve the lives of your customers and/or prospects? Share them.

When your audience learns from you, when they gain knowledge from just being associated with you (even before they've bought anything from you)...THEN they are much more likely to trust you, to reach out to you when they have a problem.

I had a prospect share with me recently that after reading through one of our weekly emails, he had learned more from that one email than from his current web company over the past two years!

This stuff really does work!

—— **CHAPTER 21** ——

My Kids and Content Marketing

MY KIDS AND CONTENT MARKETING

A few years ago, a trend swept through the United States in the form of the "Rainbow Loom." If you had kids anywhere from five to 15 at the time, you know exactly what I'm talking about. They are still around, but for about six to 12 months, everywhere you went, you saw these things – seriously…EVERYWHERE!

This phenomenon involved hundreds of little dime-sized rubber bands that kids stretched over the plastic loom, twisting, bending, and wrapping every which way to make one of what seemed like a million different bracelet styles.

Our boys were 8 and 11 at the time. They would spend hours a day making these things. Mostly, they'd watch YouTube videos of other kids showing how to do a particular style. There's one little girl who must have been only 10 or 11 herself who I heard all the time on the iPad as they'd watch, pause, bend/stretch/pull, un-pause, watch, repeat…

What does this have to do with content marketing?

As I walked in the room one day as the boys were working hard on some new looming skill, I heard what appeared to be a man's voice coming from the iPad. I said, "That's the first dude I've heard teaching how to make those things."

"I think he owns a store or something that sells this stuff," Isaac, replied without lifting his head.

Now there's a perfect example of content marketing. A small

business owner who sells Rainbow Looms and little rubber bands that go with them is utilizing video to show kids how to use the loom and create different designs. Brilliant!

Many people get overwhelmed when they think of creating content – blogs, videos, white papers, etc. This guy probably spent 5 minutes creating a quick video showing how to make a rubber band bracelet.

It's not rocket science, people.

Just think about what your audience wants/needs. And give it to them. And, when it comes time to make a purchase, you'll be the one that comes to mind.

—— **CHAPTER 22** ——

RC Cars,
Hot Wheels &
Lucky Pennies

MATT WHITE

RC CARS, HOT WHEELS &
LUCKY PENNIES

My youngest son, Ian, is a pretty typical spoiled suburban child. He has a garage full of games, toys and bikes. His bedroom houses a bearded dragon and an Xbox 360. And, he spends most of his free time with his iPhone or iPad Mini.

For Christmas a couple years ago, Ian was subtly introduced to the world of Remote Control (RC) vehicles, as he got an RC half-car-half-plane thing and an RC helicopter.

The helicopter was supposed to be able to do tricks – flip over in mid-air – but we couldn't figure out how. So, in his 9-year-old, iPad-using ways, he did a quick search on YouTube, and life as he knew it would never be the same. Not only did he uncover the secret to flipping his helicopter, but he also was exposed to the world of content marketing! (And he didn't even know it!)

A great example of content marketing.

One YouTube channel that seemed to resonate was from RCSparks.com, aka "RC Adventures." Every one of the videos is nicely done, but not overly produced. It's basically a guy (who we've now come to know as Aaron Bidochka) either talking about RC cars – sharing his thoughts on all the things he's learned (and is learning) about RC vehicles – or showing his cars, trucks, plows, motorcycles, or boats in action.

You can find Aaron and RC Adventures on YouTube at http://bit.ly/1UTu6TJ (At the time of this writing, Aaron has more than one million subscribers to his YouTube channel.)

In the weeks following Christmas, Ian watched hundreds, or possibly thousands, of videos about RC cars – mostly from RC Adventures. Any free time he had was spent with the iPad, watching RC snow plows, RC boats, RC races, discussions about RC cars, how they work, why some are different than others.

Still to this day, he spends hours each week checking out RC videos – mostly from RC Adventures. And, the next best thing he enjoys besides watching these videos by himself is…watching these videos with me! And, I've actually come to enjoy them, and the time I get to spend with him watching. (In fact, just last month I actually bought my own RC car – something I've wanted since I was Ian's age!)

RC Adventures (and Aaron Bidochka, in particular) is absolutely helping, not selling.

What's awesome about RC Adventures is that he NEVER sells anything in his videos – at least not that I've seen in all the videos I've viewed. I don't even think there's any kind of official sponsor, other than the RCSparks.com community/forum website, although there are the typical YouTube ads (of which he's clearly making some money).

The guy is just genuinely having a great time sharing what he knows. You can tell he loves every minute of it. It's a passion for him that's turned into a business. And, I think that's what attracts Ian (and apparently a million other kids and adults alike) to these videos. They're entertaining and educating, without being a sales pitch. However, even if he's now worked out some product placement opportunities, he has built up credibility with his audience. If he recommends a particular model or part, it's sure to get noticed.

RC Adventures is not the only content marketing that's reaching Ian.

As he's spent time on YouTube, he has also come across several other great examples of content marketing with video.

RaceGrooves.com

This guy reviews and "plays with" all sorts of Hot Wheels and Matchbox cars. As with RC Adventures, Ian loves watching this guy's videos. They're honest and fun – and clean for a kid to watch. And, just like RC Adventures, as far as I can tell, the content isn't sponsored. Clearly, the Hot Wheels and Matchbox brands are promoted, but not in a cheesy advertising kind of way. And, just like RC Adventures, he's also clearly making money on YouTube ads, and there are sponsors/advertisements on the Race Grooves website itself. (Find Race Grooves on YouTube at http://bit.ly/1pZVT8P)

Lucky Penny Shop

A much more direct connection to its own bottom line, the Lucky Penny Shop, a toy store in Amarillo, Texas, has a YouTube channel that reviews all kinds of toys. With more than 1.6 million subscribers as of this writing, Lucky Penny has done an awesome job of building an audience by offering helpful information. Again, I'm amazed at how captivated Ian can be with these videos; but as I watch with him from time to time (or just hear it in the background), it's clear again that the content is both entertaining and informative. (On YouTube at http://bit.ly/1RGHKWU)

So, your audience is probably not pre-teen kids.

This is not an age thing or an industry thing or even a specific product or service thing. Helping instead of traditional selling works across the board.

When you become a trusted resource for your target audience, they are more likely to buy from you.

Storytelling as a Content Marketing Tactic

When my daughter, Audrey, was much younger, I used to lay in bed with her at bedtime. We'd talk about what was good during that day and what she looked forward to most about tomorrow. Sometimes we'd read a book (a favorite was "Designed by God, So I Must Be Special" – I could recite that book, by the way!), and then sometimes she'd ask me to tell a story – one that I'd make up.

Most times, I'd intertwine something about a little girl so she'd feel a part of the story. They wouldn't last long – maybe 2-3 minutes – but Audrey would be entranced. She'd either be looking directly at me, hanging on my every word; or she'd sometimes close her eyes as she imagined the story in her mind.

Storytelling is a powerful thing.

Whether it's a child listening to her dad or you or me watching a movie of any kind, stories compel us. They pull us in and get us involved. We want to believe stories. We want to be a part of stories.

That's why telling a story should be a big part of your content marketing strategy. When you tell a story, you are more likely to grab the interest of your audience. You gain an emotional foothold and make it easier for your audience to relate to you and your product or service.

Syed Balkhi shares at least three benefits of storytelling in his article, "The Power of Storytelling: Content Strategy Tweaks Businesses Can Implement Today" (http://huff.to/1q9rzs2):

1. Telling Your Story Humanizes Your Brand
2. Stories Help Your Audience Better Understand Complex Ideas
3. Stories Help Establish Your Authority

And, in this article, Brittney Ervin from Inbound Marketing Agents shares "5 Tips for Mastering the Art of Brand Storytelling" (http://bit.ly/1UvlKSL).

Remember, your stories shouldn't be all about you. Share stories about your clients. Tell stories about your industry. Use stories to explain why your product or service helped save a life, improve the bottom line or increase X.

And, just like when I would share a bedtime story with Audrey, be sure to embed your audience into the story whenever possible. When your prospect can envision herself in your story, you have a much better chance of connecting with her.

What's your story?

Are you telling a story with your marketing, or are you just talking about your company, product or service?

—— **CHAPTER 23** ——

H is for
Holy $@!%

MATT WHITE

H is for
Holy $@!%

I'm not much of a cussing kind of guy. In fact, when I was a kid, any time I had to spell my name out loud, I would say "M – A – double T" because I thought "tee-tee" (otherwise known as "pee-pee") was a bad word. Now, with kids of my own, I do my best to explain that "words are just words. It's all in how you use those words that makes the difference." And, I think it's working, as Ian (10) loves singing with Zac Brown Band: *"I got my toes in the water, ASS in the sand…"* and he's thrilled that he can say the word "ass" without getting in trouble!

(One caveat – you'll notice I still steered away from using the actual word "shit" in the title of this chapter…that would take things one step too far, in my opinion. Plus, my mom, who is proofreading this book along the way, would probably kill over right on the spot! Sorry mom. *I'll be sure to wash my own mouth out with soap when I get home tonight.)*

While I still believe it's mostly not necessary, I agree with Guy Kawasaki (in his book *Enchantment*) when he says there's a time and place for strong language…mostly when it's related to making a point or showing emotion or passion about something.

And THIS is where I circle back to what this chapter is all about. H is the first letter in the word HELP. It's also the first letter of the H.E.L.P. acronym that explains the process one goes through when he first begins to open his eyes to the idea of helping versus selling.

H is for Holy #@!%

I've experienced it myself, and I've seen it happen with my clients. Once you begin to look at your business (and life, in general) as a means of helping people, there's this a-ha moment when it clicks — and you really have that feeling of "Holy #@!%, this makes sense."

- o You start to see opportunity where you hadn't seen it before.
- o You begin to recognize that some of the brands you love the most are doing this same thing — and that's why you love them so much.
- o It's like you had blinders on — blinders that only allowed you to focus on "selling" something…eeking out a few more dollars per sale, getting a new customer at all costs, selling another product, upselling current clients, etc.
- o And you start to wonder how in the world you missed this. How could such a simple concept go unnoticed for so long?

E is for Everywhere

I recently bought a Ram 1500 Big Horn truck. It's a massive thing; and I never pictured myself as a "truck guy," but now I love it. And, you know what kind of vehicle I see EVERYWHERE now? Ram 1500 Big Horns! There's actually a "phenomenon" for this. It's called the Baader-Meinhof Phenomenon, and it's defined by Wikipedia as "the illusion in which a word, a name, or other thing that has recently come to one's attention suddenly seems to appear with improbable frequency shortly afterwards." This same phenomenon happens when your mindset changes to one of helping from one of selling.

Helping in a Meeting…

Now, when you walk into a meeting with a first-time prospect, your mindset is completely different. You're there to help that person, not sell them something. So, the conversation goes in a completely different direction than it would have in the past. You're asking questions, good questions, to find out if you can help. And, if you can't, that's okay; you'll find someone else to help. But, if you can, all the better.

Helping Online…

Now, when you go to write a blog, you write in such a way that offers helpful information for your customers and prospects, not another sales pitch about another feature of your product. You create content with the reader in mind, rather than your company in mind. Instead of posting a link to *your* website from Twitter, you share a link to another website that you think might help your audience (yes, maybe even a competitor's website!).

Helping in Person...

Now, when you have lunch with a friend or co-worker or client, you find yourself genuinely interested in what's going on in their life or business situation. You don't jump in with a quick solution, because you're listening well. You have the other person's interests in mind. Maybe there's a way you can help; and maybe there's not. Helping may just come in the form of listening.

L is for Listening & Responding

When you change from an attitude of A.B.C. (Always Be Closing) to an attitude of H.E.L.P., you start listening more. You begin to listen and look for ways to help your prospect, your co-worker, your neighbor, your friend. Your respond with genuine compassion and a desire to see the other person succeed, instead of doing everything you can to turn it into a "win" for yourself.

P is for Profit

I've said it time and time again throughout this book: the bottom line is still part of the equation. And the last letter in the H.E.L.P. acronym is a P for PROFIT. People recognize that you're actually there to help them, and not just trying to push your product or service on them. This establishes credibility and increased trust among your peers, your clients, and your prospects. And that ultimately turns into better relationships, stronger connections, and more business.

Simple, Yet Powerful

The concept of helping isn't a difficult one. It's just often overlooked. But, once employed, it can be one of the most powerful concepts in your arsenal.

—— **CHAPTER 24** ——

Generosity: 3 Reasons Why It's Essential to Your Business

MATT WHITE

GENEROSITY: 3 REASONS WHY IT'S ESSENTIAL TO YOUR BUSINESS

Generosity.

What do you think of when you read/hear this word?

I'm guessing there's not a bad thought that even comes close to entering your mind.

Here are three reasons **why generosity is essential to your success...**

1. To my first point, generosity is, by default, a positive concept. Those who are generous are generally perceived as "better" people. The opposite is also true. When you're selfish, it shows. Nobody likes to do business with someone who thinks of no one but himself.

2. When you are generous with your time, talents and financial resources, the world benefits. Whether it's literally "the world" through financial donations to organizations that help around the globe or "your world" because you spend time leading a local Boy Scout troop, your impact on the world around you is positive. In your workplace, being generous works to the benefit of everyone – the project gets done faster; the ideas are better with more input; the intern learns something new; the customer feels good about working with your business. **Everyone wins.**

3. What goes around, comes around. When you're generous, others are much more likely to be generous with you. It's also a fact that being generous leads others to do the same. It's terrible that I can't remember the bank's name, but there was a great series of TV commercials from a bank that showed one person doing something nice for another. A seemingly unrelated person noticed that act of generosity or kindness and in turn helped someone else out. This chain of events goes on and on through seven or eight circumstances. When we see someone being generous, we're more likely to be generous ourselves and vice versa.

Find some area to be generous today.

CONCLUSION

Something happened in a meeting today that will help wrap up this whole book. It's funny how timing works just right, isn't it?

"People want to see what we do first; and then, if they like what they see, they'll want to learn more about us."

This statement came from a prospect in a meeting where we were talking about how (or even if) the company's website should focus more on the pictures and what they do instead of helping to address the questions, concerns and "pains" of their prospective customers.

She said, "I've looked at probably 100 websites of our competitors and others in our industry, and they all have pretty pictures and very few words on the home page."

To add to the irony of the timing of today being the day I write this conclusion AND have this conversation with this prospect, this morning I happened to put out a video titled, "Are You a Purple Cow?" (http://bit.ly/1N5xVO4). It was basically a recommendation to read Seth Godin's book, *Purple Cow*.

The gist of the story goes like this: Nothing is special about a brown cow. You see them all the time. Especially when you're on a long driving trip, you see hundreds, if not thousands, of brown cows. And, the more you see, the less you pay attention to them.

However, if you're driving down the highway, and you notice a purple cow standing out in the pasture, that's going to grab your attention. That is going to make you take a second look.

At the beginning of this book, I mention the fact that consumers (buyers, in general) have so many options. What that really means is there are tons of brown cows out there. The people, businesses and organizations that stand out are going to be the ones who win.

Do you want to stand out?

As this person described the hundred or so websites that all offered basically the same thing, I said, "Don't you think that if you were a potential customer, and you had clicked through three, five or ten of these other websites, and then landed on one that was different – one that, instead of "selling" you right away with pretty pictures and very little content, it addressed your exact frustration or answered the question you couldn't get resolved from any other resource out there – don't you think THAT one would stand out?"

I asked her how she would go about buying a TV. I asked what would be the first thing she'd do? Her answer: "I'd go Google and search for 'best TV reviews.'" I dug a little more, asking her what she would do next. "I would do some research, find out which TV was the best, which had the highest ratings, the best resolution, that kind of stuff."

Then, I asked her one more question: "If you did all the research, and there was one website that had given you a ton of great information and educated you on which TV was best and why...wouldn't you be more likely to buy a TV from that company than the one that just showed a picture of the TV with a price beside it?"

What do you think her answer was? "Yah. I guess I would."

When it comes do to the core of every one of us, we would rather be helped than "sold." We would rather be educated than talked at or manipulated. We would rather be entertained than bored with details we don't care about.

So, here's my charge to you: Stop selling, and start helping instead. And watch how your business grows!

ABOUT THE AUTHOR

Matt White has been an entrepreneur ever since he can remember. What he loves most about entrepreneurship is the part where he gets to help people – business owners, start-ups, marketing folks, other entrepreneurs. From black-market "reminders" in the fifth grade to developing online marketing programs for all types of clients today, his focus has always been on helping people.

Now president of JoltCMS (JoltCMS.com) and The Remodeler's Edge (TheRemodelersEdge.com), as well as the founder of Remodeler Marketing Institute (RemodelerMarketingInstitute.com), Matt gets to help a variety of business owners and entrepreneurs every single day.

He speaks across the country, leading everything from small workshops and conference breakout sessions (30-45 minutes) to educational seminars (60-90 minutes) to TED-style talks (less than 20 minutes). His ***Stop Selling. Start Helping.*** concept rings true no matter the industry or audience – from corporate sales teams and franchisees/dealers to national associations and trade groups.

To book Matt for your conference, workshop, trade show or other event, visit www.JoltCMS.com/speaking.

Made in the USA
Charleston, SC
01 December 2016